Gifts
to Make for
Your Favorite
Grownup

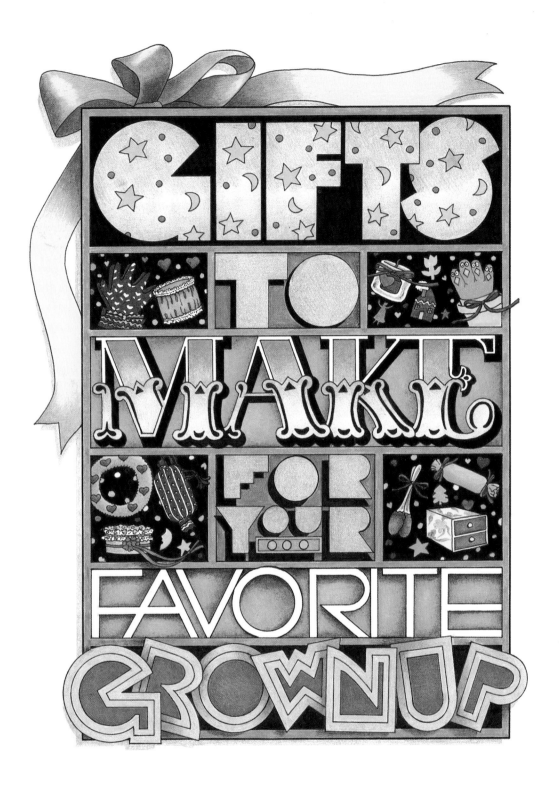

Kathy Ross

Illustrated by Anne Canevari Green

The Millbrook Press
Brookfield, Connecticut

To Tom, who likes things neat, but doesn't
complain when my projects fill the house.—K.R.

To Monte, who also likes things neat, and <u>does</u>
complain when my projects fill the house.—A.C.G.

Published by The Millbrook Press, Inc.
2 Old New Milford Road
Brookfield, Connecticut 06804

Copyright © 1996 by Kathy Ross
Illustrations copyright © 1996 by Anne Canevari Green
All rights reserved
Printed in the United States of America

1 3 5 6 4 2

Library of Congress Cataloging-in-Publication Data
Ross, Kathy (Katharine Reynolds), 1948-
Gifts to make for your favorite grownup/Kathy Ross:
illustrated by Anne Canevari Green.
p.   cm.
Includes bibliographical references and index.
Summary: Provides instructions for making fifty crafts
suitable as gifts for adults.
ISBN 1-56294-274-3 (lib. bdg.) 0-7613-0079-1 (pbk.)
1. Handicraft—Juvenile literature.   2. Recycling (Waste, etc.)—
Juvenile literature.   3. Gifts—Juvenile literature.
[1. Handicraft.   2. Gifts.]   I. Green, Anne Canevari, ill.
II. Title.
TT160.R71423   1996
745.5—dc20   95-50294 CIP AC

Contents

Hi Kids!

If you are reading this book you must like to make things. I have loved crafts of all kinds for as long as I can remember. I like to look at things that other people are going to throw away and think of different ways to turn them into something new.

This craft book is full of ideas for things you can make to give as gifts to all the grownups in your life. They are attractive and useful items. Most important, they are things that you really can make! Handmade gifts are a fun and thoughtful way to show someone that you care.

Here are some helpful things you should know before you get started:

- These crafts do not require exact measurements. When I give measurements, it is only to give you some idea of the size of the finished project I made. If your measurements are not exactly the same as mine, the project will still work out fine.

- These crafts do not require unusual or hard-to-find items. Most projects can be made with things you have around the house. As you gather materials for each project, please remember to ask the adult in your house if it is all right for you to use the items.

- These crafts do not require you to use any dangerous tools or toxic adhesives. Every craft in this book can be made with white glue. In some projects I list blue glue gel because it will be easier to use for that project. Blue glue gel is a thick, tacky glue that does not run or drip the way white glue does. This means that your pieces will stay where you want them even when the glue is wet. If you do not have blue glue gel, white glue will also work.

- I often tell you to dry your projects on a Styrofoam tray or plastic wrap. This is so your project will not stick to the surface it is drying on if some of the glue drips. If you leave a gluey project to dry on newspaper, you might end up with bits of newspaper stuck to the bottom of the project. (Be sure to always wash cups, spoons, and paintbrushes right away after using glue.)

- For several projects I tell you to cover the surface of a material with masking tape. White glue will not stick to certain surfaces, such as plastic and metal, but it will stick to the tape covering and hold the pieces together.

- When you choose a gift that you would like to make, collect enough materials to make more than one. This gives you a chance to practice before you make the gift you'll give away. You can also experiment and add some ideas of your own.

Use your imagination when making all the gifts in this book to find new ways to use, change, and decorate the basic crafts. I wish I could hear about all the different ways you'll discover!
Have fun!

Kathy Ross

Gifts for Growing Things

Designer Planter

This designer planter is a terrific way to display your artistic talents.

Here is what you need:

two disposable clear plastic cups of the same size

scissors

cellophane tape

white glue

masking tape

colored markers

pretty trim and ribbon

white typing paper

Here is what you do:

Wrap the piece of white paper around the outside of one of the cups and hold it in place with a small piece of tape. Trim away the excess paper above and below the cup. Carefully remove the tape and neatly cut away all but about 1 inch (2.5 centimeters) of the overlap of paper along the side of the cup. You should now have a piece of paper that fits neatly inside one of the cups. If it still does not quite fit, trim away any excess paper so that it does.

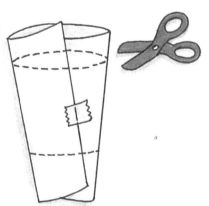

Put the paper liner down flat on a table and decorate it with markers. Make sure that your design will be right side up when you put it back into the cup. You might want to write a message on the paper to the person you are making this for.

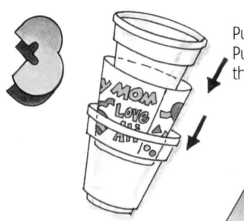

Put the decorated paper back inside the cup. Put the other cup inside the first cup so that the paper is between the two cups.

Tape the rims of both cups with masking tape to seal out any moisture from the plant. Cover the tape with glue and one or more rows of pretty trim and ribbon.

You can drop a pre-potted plant inside this planter or plant some seeds or a plant directly in it.

If you are making more than one planter, or think you might want to make more later, trace around the paper that you cut to fit inside the cup. You can use this tracing as a pattern for each planter you make, as long as you use the same kind of cup each time.

N apkin Flower Pot

You can make beautiful flower pots with the colorful paper napkins found in many gift stores. Make sure the napkins have a pattern all over them rather than a picture in just one section.

Here is what you need:

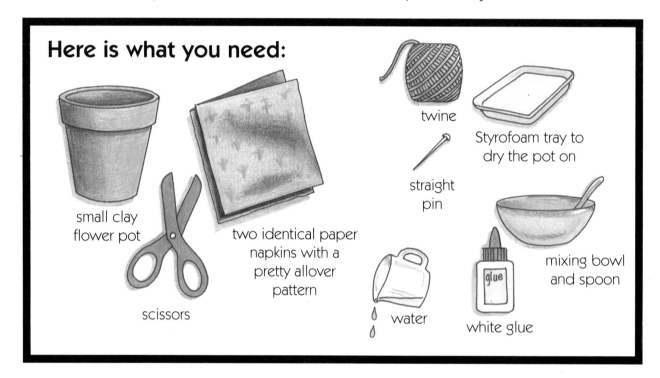

small clay flower pot

scissors

two identical paper napkins with a pretty allover pattern

twine

straight pin

water

Styrofoam tray to dry the pot on

white glue

mixing bowl and spoon

Here is what you do:

Make sure that the clay pot is clean and dry. It does not need to be a new pot. Cracks and chips will not show in the finished project.

Pour 3/4 cup (175 milliliters) of white glue into a bowl and add about 1/4 cup (50 milliliters) of water. Mix the glue and water well with a spoon.

12

You will cover the pot with one or two napkins, depending on the size of the pot. Open the napkins and see how you need to place them in order to cover the pot completely. Turn the pot upside down in the sink.

Dip one napkin in the watery glue to completely cover both sides of the napkin with the mixture. Carefully lift the napkin out of the glue and drape it over the bottom and one side of the pot. Lift the pot so that you can fold the ends of the napkin into it. Do the same thing with a second napkin to cover the pot completely. Work carefully. This is very messy to do, because the watery glue runs all over the place. If the napkin tears, patch the spot with a gluey piece of another napkin. It will look fine when it dries.

Carefully pat the napkins down over the pot so that there are no air bubbles between the pot and the napkins. If there are some you can't get rid of, pop them with the pin. Shape the napkins tightly over the rim of the pot.

Cut a piece of twine about 18 inches (46 centimeters) long. Tie the twine in a bow around the pot just under the rim. Turn the pot upside down on the Styrofoam tray and let it dry completely. This could take as long as two days.

Be sure to wash the bowl, spoon, and sink as soon as you have finished the project. You will probably need to wash yourself, too!

lastic Watering Jug

This watering jug is the perfect gift for a person with lots of house plants to take care of.

Here is what you need:

package of five colors of self-stick plastic labeling tape

scissors

1-gallon (4-liter) plastic milk or cider jug

Here is what you do:

Make a flower or other design on each side of the plastic jug with pieces of the labeling tape. (It is easier to peel the backing off part of the strip while it is still on the roll, then cut the pieces you need for the design and stick them on the jug. If you cut the pieces first and try to peel each piece separately, it is harder to do and takes more time.)

Hint: Don't use a plastic jug that contained soap or another cleaner. If the jug isn't clean, the liquid could harm the plants.

You will probably have enough tape to decorate more than one watering jug, depending on how fancy your decoration is.

ag Clip

These bag clips keep snacks fresh and crisp by holding the bag closed once it has been opened. Make several clips at one time and keep them on hand for when you need a special little gift in a hurry.

Here is what you need:

Styrofoam tray to dry the clips on

white glue

wooden clamp clothespins— one for each bag clip you wish to make

colored markers

paintbrush

MACARONI
box of alphabet macaroni

Here is what you do:

For each clip you wish to make, color the two flat sides of the clothespin with one or more markers.

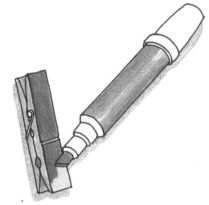

Decide what you would like to write on the clip. It could be the name of the person you plan to give it to or something funny like "yum yum" or "keep out." It could also be the name of a special snack you know that person likes to eat. Once you decide, find the macaroni letters you will need and set them aside.

Carefully place the letters on one side of the clothespin to see how you want to arrange them. Take the letters off and set them aside again. Use the paintbrush to cover one flat side of the clothespin with glue. If you did not use a permanent marker, the color may run a little, so do this with as few strokes of the brush as possible so that the color is not washed off. When the glue is dry, it will protect the color from moisture.

Arrange the macaroni letters on top of the wet glue and place the project, letters up, on a Styrofoam tray to dry.

Cover the back of the clothespin and the letters on the front of the clothespin with a thin layer of glue for protection. Set the clothespin on its side on the Styrofoam tray so that the two sides with glue on them are not touching the tray. Let the glue dry.

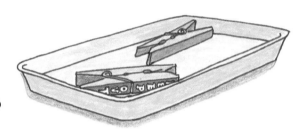

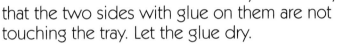

Put three or four of these clips in a sandwich bag and tie the top with pretty yarn or ribbon. You might even want to give a bag of chips or other snack with the clips to add to the surprise.

If you add a piece of sticky-backed magnet to the back of each bag clip, they can be stored on the refrigerator when they are not being used.

r. Blueberry String Holder

This happy blueberry is really a storage container for string.

Here is what you need:

blue, red, white, and green construction paper

ball of string

plastic drinking straw

large oatmeal box

scissors

pencil

cellophane tape

white glue

Here is what you do:

Cut off the top of the oatmeal box so that you have a box 4 inches (10 centimeters) tall. The box should be large enough for a ball of string to fit in, with enough room left to put the lid back on the box.

Hint: If you have a very large ball of string, make the box a little taller so that the string will fit inside. Place the ball of string in the oatmeal box before you cut it so you'll be sure the box is the right size.

 Cut blue paper to fit around the outside of the box. Glue the paper in place and hold the ends together with tape while the glue dries. Cut a circle of blue paper to cover the lid of the box and glue it on. Cut a smile out of red paper and eyes from white and blue paper. Glue them on the blue lid to make a face.

 Put the lid on the box and turn the box on its side so that the face is facing you. Cut a pointy leaf from green paper and glue it on top of the blueberry box.

 Cut a 3-inch (7.5-centimeter) piece of plastic straw. Poke a hole in the middle of the leaf and stick the straw partway through the hole. Use tape to secure the straw on the inside of the box.

Put the ball of string inside the box and thread the end of the string up through the straw. Put the lid back on the box and turn the box on its side with the end of the string coming out of the stem at the top of the blueberry.

The string holder does not have to be a blueberry. It could be a pumpkin, apple, or some other kind of round fruit or vegetable. It could also be a person or an animal. What other things can you think of to make into a string holder?

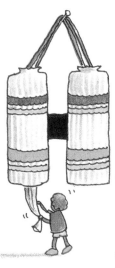

anging Plastic Bag Keeper

There are plenty of uses for plastic grocery bags, but where do you keep them all until you need them? Make this handy bag keeper for someone.

Hint: Knee socks or tube socks work well for this project.

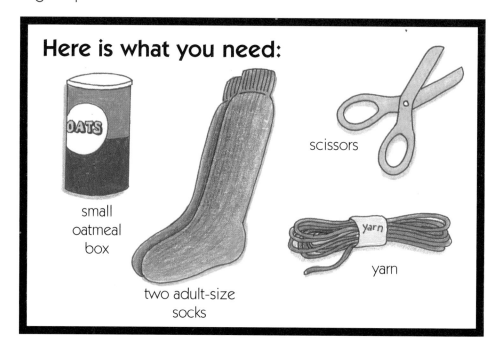

Here is what you need:

small oatmeal box

two adult-size socks

scissors

yarn

Here is what you do:

Remove the lid from the top of the oatmeal box. Cut the bottom out of the box so that you have a tube that is open at both ends.

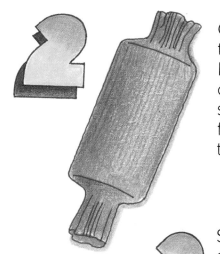

Cut the foot off of one sock. Slide the sock over the box so that there is a tight cuff at each end. If the sock is not stretchy enough to make a tight cuff on the cut end, cut the foot off of a second sock and slide that sock over the cut end of the first sock. The cuff of the second sock will be at the opposite end from the cuff of the first sock.

Slide down the cuff at one end of the box so that you can poke four holes, equally spaced, around the rim of the box. Tie the end of a 7-inch (18-centimeter) piece of yarn through each hole. Knot the ends of the four pieces of yarn together to form a hanger for the box. Pull the cuff back up around the yarn.

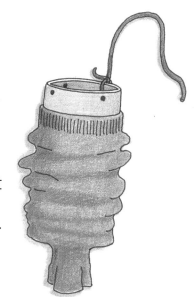

 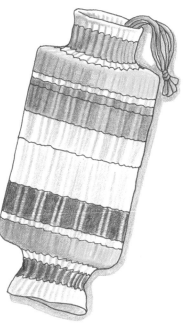

If the socks are patterned and very colorful, you may feel the bag holder looks fine and is ready to fill with bags. If the holder looks too plain, glue pieces of yarn on it to decorate it with the word "BAGS."

Fill the bag holder from the top. Hold the bags in at the bottom as you push in as many as it can hold. Bags can be pulled out through the bottom cuff as they are needed. No home should be without one!

21

Dirty or Clean Dishwasher Magnet

Everyone with a dishwasher will be glad to have this magnet. It will help them remember if the dishes in the dishwasher have been washed or not.

Here is what you need:

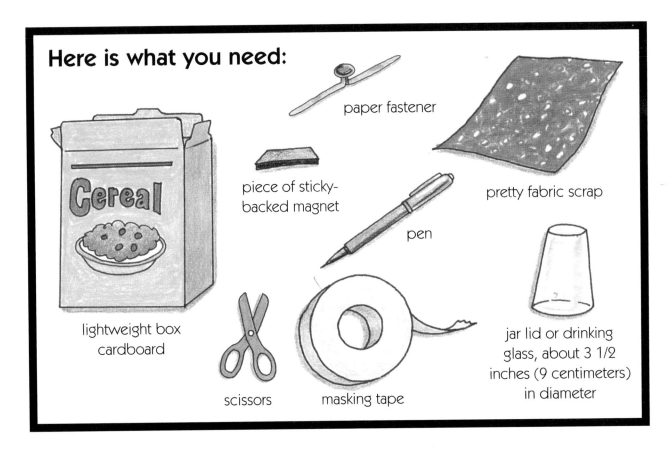

paper fastener

piece of sticky-backed magnet

pretty fabric scrap

pen

Cereal

lightweight box cardboard

scissors

masking tape

jar lid or drinking glass, about 3 1/2 inches (9 centimeters) in diameter

Here is what you do:

Trace two identical circles on the cardboard using the glass or jar lid as a pattern. Cut one circle out. Cut around the other circle about 1/2 inch (1.25 centimeters) away from the edge of the tracing line.

22

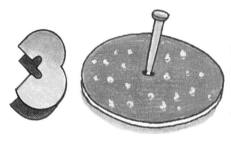

Turn the larger circle over so that the outline of the circle is face down. Cover the back with glue and a pretty piece of fabric and let it dry. When it is dry, turn the cardboard over again and cut out the traced circle.

Set the fabric-covered circle on top of the cardboard circle so that the edges exactly match. Poke a hole in the middle of the circles and hold them together with a paper fastener.

Take the two circles apart. Cut a piece out of the fabric-covered circle above the hole for the paper fastener that will be big enough to show the words "clean" and "dirty" on the back circle. Put the two circles back together with the paper fastener and write "clean" on the part of the back circle that shows. Turn the back circle so that the word "clean" is hidden behind the fabric. Now write the word "dirty" on the part of the back circle that shows. Attach a piece of sticky-backed magnet to the back circle.

This magnet can be left on the front of the dishwasher. If the dishwasher is not yet full enough to wash the dishes inside, turn the magnet to "dirty." If the dishes inside are washed and ready to be unloaded, turn the magnet to "clean."

Give someone this clever gift to help avoid confusion over clean and dirty dishes.

elping Hands Napkin Holder

These helping hands will be a welcome addition to the kitchen of someone who thinks you are very special. Grownups love to get gifts made from the outline of your hands.

Here is what you need:

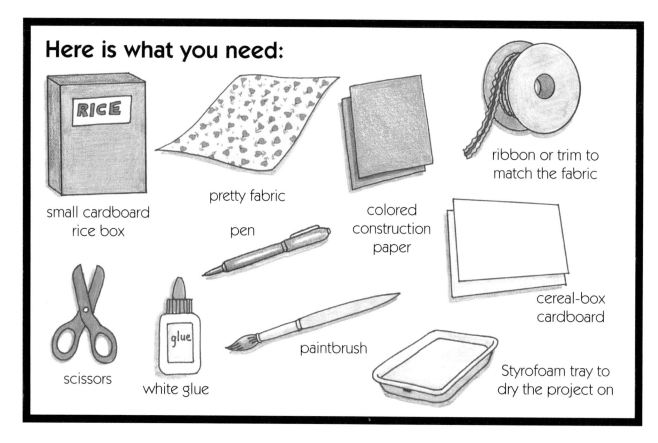

small cardboard rice box

pretty fabric

pen

scissors

white glue

paintbrush

colored construction paper

ribbon or trim to match the fabric

cereal-box cardboard

Styrofoam tray to dry the project on

Here is what you do:

Cut off the top of the box so that you have a box about 1 1/2 inches (4 centimeters) tall. Cut a 1-inch (2.5-centimeter) piece out of the two narrow sides, leaving 1/2-inch-high (1.25-centimeter) sides for support. This will be the base for the napkin holder.

Cut construction paper to cover the inner and outer surfaces of the base and glue the paper in place.

Cut out the front or back of the cereal box. Make sure that this cardboard is big enough to trace both of your hands on. If it is not, you will need to cover both sides of two pieces of cardboard with fabric instead of just one piece of cardboard.

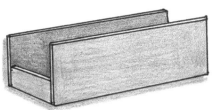

Use a paintbrush to spread a thin layer of glue evenly over one side of the cardboard. Press the fabric down over the glue, smoothing it out with your fingers so that it will dry without air bubbles between the fabric and the cardboard. Do the same thing with the other side of the cardboard. Let the glue dry.

Trace around both of your hands on the fabric-covered cardboard and cut the hands out. On the outside of the napkin holder, glue the wrist portion of one hand to each side of the base. Glue trim or ribbon around the bottom of the holder and glue a bow at the base of each hand.

Fill this holder with paper napkins and give it to someone who loves you a lot. This project also makes a very nice letter holder.

If you have some large scraps of fabric-covered cardboard left, you can use them to make the Dirty or Clean Dishwasher Magnet on page 20.

Rope Trivet

Trivets, pads that are used to protect the table from hot dishes, are always welcome and much-used gifts.

Here is what you need:

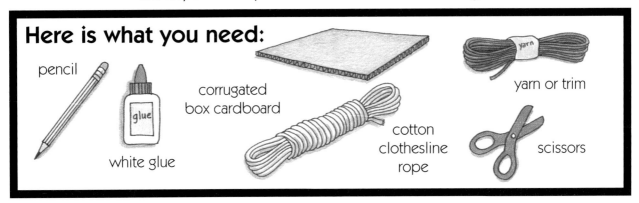

pencil

white glue

corrugated box cardboard

cotton clothesline rope

yarn or trim

scissors

Here is what you do:

To make the pattern, find a plate that is the size you would like the trivet to be. Trace around the plate on the corrugated cardboard. Do not cut out the circle yet.

Cover the cardboard circle with glue. Starting at the center of the circle, carefully coil the rope around and around itself until the circle is completely covered. Cut off the excess rope and let the project dry completely. The coil of rope will probably not fit the circle exactly. That's okay.

When the glue has dried, cut around the circle of rope as close to the edge as possible. Cover the outer edge of the circle with glue, then wrap the edge with colorful yarn or trim.

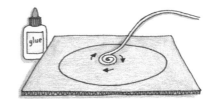

Once you have made this circle trivet, try some of these other ideas. You could change the shape of the trivet to a square or rectangle. You could make a set of four small circles to use as coasters.

26

Gifts for
the Desk

Necktie Pencil Can

This pencil can made from old neckties makes a handsome addition to any desk. Each pencil can you make will be a one-of-a-kind creation because there is an endless variety of old neckties available.

Here is what you need:

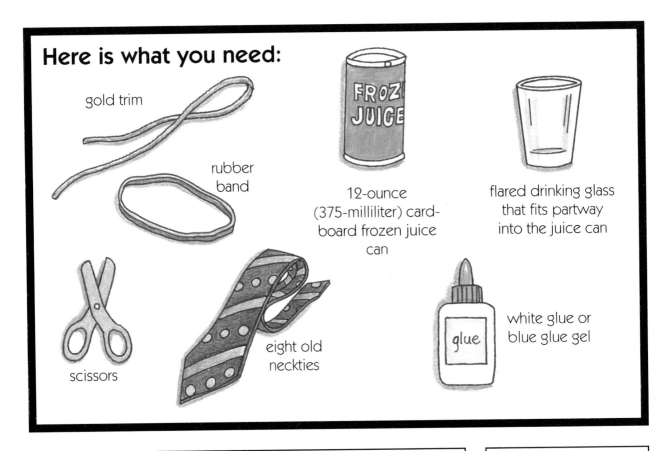

gold trim

rubber band

12-ounce (375-milliliter) cardboard frozen juice can

flared drinking glass that fits partway into the juice can

scissors

eight old neckties

white glue or blue glue gel

Hint: When I told people I needed old neckties for my craft projects, I could not believe the response! I have cartons of them in my cellar waiting to be made into other things. The necktie fabrics are often very beautiful and always interesting. Ask the adults that you know if they can help you find some old ties. I'll bet you will have a collection like mine before you know it.

Hint: If the juice can you are using is plastic instead of cardboard, cover it with masking tape to create a surface that the glue will stick to.

Here is what you do:

 Choose eight neckties in a combination of patterns that you think look good together. Measuring from the point of the thin end of one tie, cut a piece 6 inches (15 centimeters) long. Do the same with each tie.

Cover the can with white glue or blue glue gel. The glue gel is thicker than white glue so it is easier to use with fabric. Glue the tie pieces, with their points up, around the juice can to cover it.

Rub glue around the inside edge of the can and fold all the points of the ties into the can. Put a drinking glass partway down into the can to hold the points in place until the glue dries. Put a rubber band around the bottom of the can to hold the ties in place while the glue is drying. When the glue has dried, remove the glass and the rubber band.

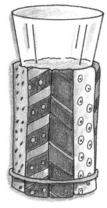

Cut a piece of gold trim to fit around the bottom of the can and glue it in place.

Be sure to save the other ends of the cut neckties for other projects. You might want to make the Glasses Holder on page 62.

29

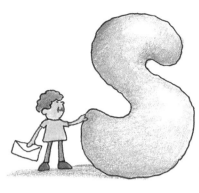

Sticker Seals

These sticker seals make a nice surprise to enclose when writing a note to someone. Make lots of them at once—some to give as gifts and some to enclose in your own thank-you notes and letters.

Here is what you need:

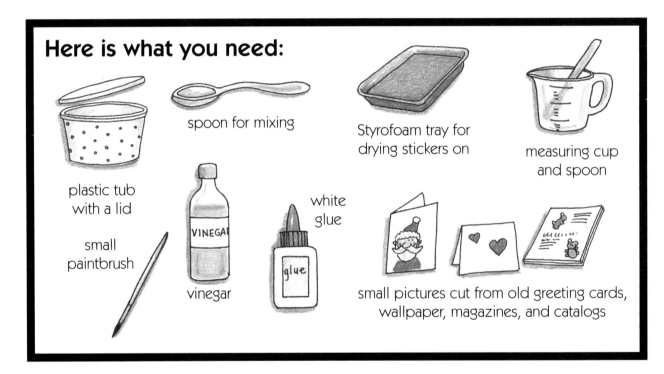

plastic tub with a lid

spoon for mixing

Styrofoam tray for drying stickers on

measuring cup and spoon

small paintbrush

white glue

vinegar

small pictures cut from old greeting cards, wallpaper, magazines, and catalogs

Here is what you do:

 Mix about 1/4 cup (50 milliliters) of white glue with one table-spoon (15 milliliters) of vinegar in a plastic tub. Mix the glue and vinegar well.

Cut tiny, sticker-size pictures from the cards, catalogs, magazines, or wallpaper you have collected. Cut around the pictures carefully, getting as close to the edges as you can.

Brush the back of each picture with the glue mixture. Let the pictures dry face down on a Styrofoam tray.

When the stickers are dry, they will be ready to use when needed. Just wipe the back of a sticker with a damp sponge and stick the sticker wherever you want it.

You can draw your own pictures on white paper and turn them into stickers, too. You might also want to cut small shapes such as hearts or stars from colored paper to make into stickers.

Decorated Bulletin Board Tacks

A set of decorated thumb tacks will cheer up any bulletin board. These are so attractive and easy to make you might want to make a set for yourself!

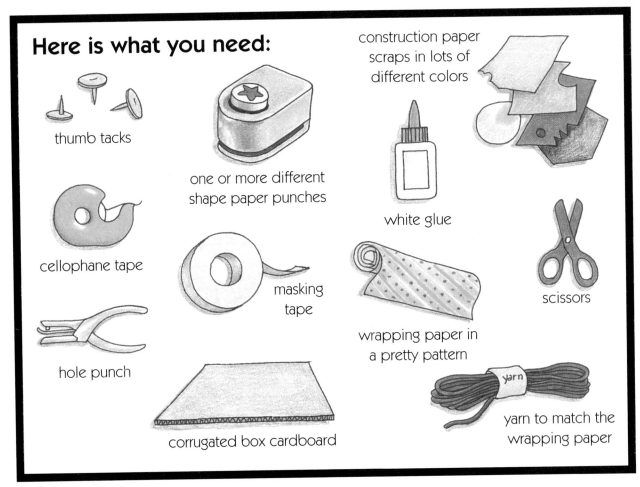

Here is what you need:

thumb tacks

one or more different shape paper punches

construction paper scraps in lots of different colors

white glue

cellophane tape

masking tape

wrapping paper in a pretty pattern

scissors

hole punch

corrugated box cardboard

yarn to match the wrapping paper

Here is what you do:

Cover the top of ten thumb tacks with a tiny piece of masking tape so that glue will stick to them. White glue does not stick well to a metal surface.

32

Punch out a pretty shape for each thumb tack. If you have lots of different shape punches, use them all. If you have just one, use lots of different colors of paper.

If you do not have any shape punches, punch holes from different colors of paper and glue them in the shapes of flowers on the top of the tacks. Use orange or yellow for the center of the flower with a pretty ring of circles in a bright color around the center to form the flower petals.

Hint: Shape paper punches come in all sorts of different shapes—stars, bears, and hearts, to name a few. But don't pass this project by because you don't have any shape paper punches. You can use a regular hole punch, too.

To make a display card for the tacks, cut a piece of cardboard about 2 1/2 inches by 4 inches (6 centimeters by 10 centimeters). Wrap the cardboard in pretty wrapping paper just as you would wrap up a gift, covering both sides. Use tape to hold the paper in place. Cut a piece of yarn for a hanger and tape the two ends on the back of the wrapped cardboard.

Push all of the tacks you made partway into the front of the wrapped cardboard. The tacks can now be hung on a bulletin board, ready to be used when needed.

You can decorate the tacks with tiny stickers, like stars. You can even draw your own pictures to glue on. Small, flat, colorful buttons might look nice glued to the tacks, too. If you use buttons, be sure to put a tiny piece of masking tape on the back of each one to help the white glue stick to the button.

# essage Holder

This message holder is just the thing for busy grownups to keep by the phone.

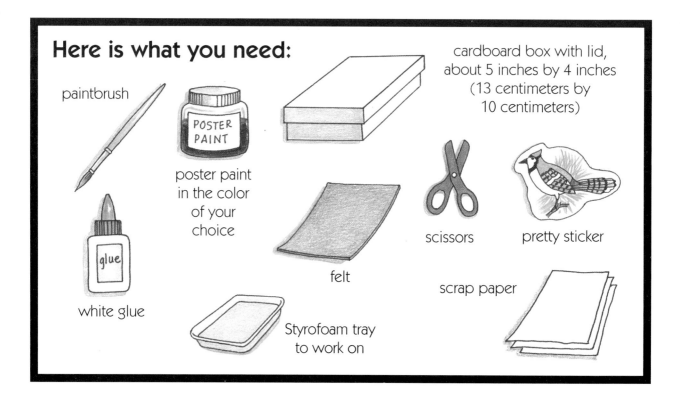

Here is what you need:

paintbrush

POSTER PAINT

poster paint in the color of your choice

white glue

Styrofoam tray to work on

felt

cardboard box with lid, about 5 inches by 4 inches (13 centimeters by 10 centimeters)

scissors

pretty sticker

scrap paper

Hint: A gift box that held a necklace, bracelet, or other piece of jewelry makes a perfect box for this project.

Hint: Your message holder can be any size you want it to be, so don't skip this project because your box is not exactly the same size as the one I used. It's important that the box is made of good, heavy cardboard and has a lid.

Here is what you do:

 Cut away about two thirds of the box lid. Glue the small remaining portion of the lid over one end of the box. This will be the paper holder.

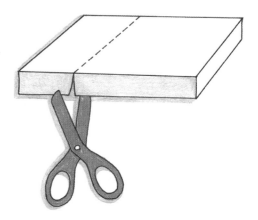

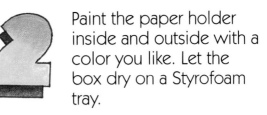
Paint the paper holder inside and outside with a color you like. Let the box dry on a Styrofoam tray.

Put a sticker on top of the lid to decorate it. Even though it is self-sticking, use glue to hold the sticker in place so that you can be sure it won't come off later.

Cover the bottom of the box with felt.

Cut scrap paper to fit inside the box and fill the box.
If you have a small pencil, put that in the box, too.

If you do not have any stickers, cut a picture from a greeting card or magazine. You could also use a school photo of yourself as decoration. If you have some small sea shells, they might look nice glued on the box, too. There are so many different ways you might decorate this project! What do you think would look nice?

35

Rubber Band Message Board

This unusual message board is useful and fun. You don't need any tacks to hang your messages with. Just tuck a pencil and lots of note paper behind the crisscross of rubber bands.

Here is what you need:

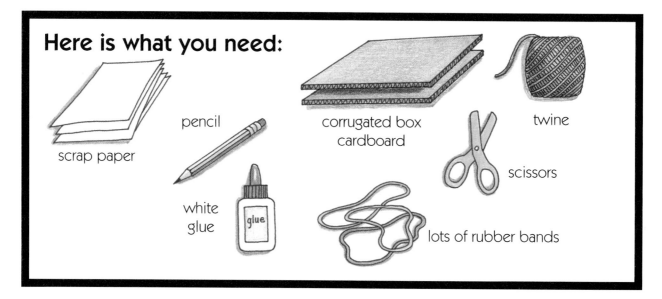

scrap paper

pencil

white glue

corrugated box cardboard

twine

scissors

lots of rubber bands

Here is what you do:

Cut four pieces of cardboard about 9 inches by 8 inches (23 centimeters by 20 centimeters). Cut an 8-inch (20-centimeter) piece of twine to use as a hanger for the board. Glue the first two pieces of cardboard together, then glue the other two pieces together.

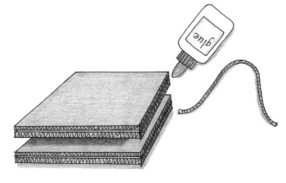

Now glue the two double pieces of cardboard together with the two ends of the twine in between them to form a hanger for the board. The several layers of cardboard make a thick, strong base for the message board so that the board will not bend from the pressure of the rubber bands.

Cover the board with a crisscross of rubber bands. Keep adding rubber bands until you are happy with the way it looks. You will need to use at least ten rubber bands to create a large enough area on the board to hold messages.

Cut a stack of scrap paper and tuck it behind some of the rubber bands. Add a pencil, and the message board is ready to give to someone you know who could use some help getting organized.

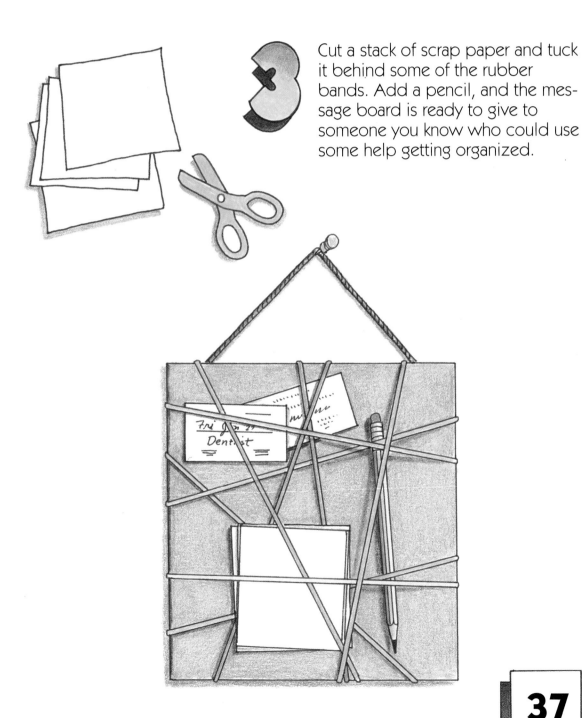

Designer Return Address Labels

This set of return-address labels of your own design makes a great gift for just about anyone. You can decorate the labels to fit the personality of the grownup you are making them for.

Hint: Remember that if the labels get wet, as mail sometimes does, regular markers will wash off. Only use permanent markers or a pen.

Here is what you need:

sharp permanent markers

pen

stickers

SELF-ADHESIVE LABELS

package of white self-adhesive labels, 1 inch by 2.75 inches (2.5 centimeters by 7 centimeters)

Here is what you do:

Find out the complete name and address of the person you are making the labels for. With a permanent marker or pen, write the name and address on four sheets of four labels each. This will make a set of sixteen return-address labels. Make sure to leave space on the left side of the label so you can add some decoration.

Draw a picture on each label with markers. You can draw the same picture on each of the labels so that it looks like a printed set, or you can draw a different picture on each one. If you do not want to draw, you can use small stickers, like foil stars, to decorate the labels instead.

Kathy Ross
100 Main Street
Anytown USA 10000

Put the set of return-address labels inside an envelope and stick one of the labels on the front of the envelope. This will not only tell who the gift is for, but will also give the lucky person a place to store the labels.

Kathy Ross
100 Main Street
Anytown USA 10000

Gifts for
the Closet
and Bath

Hanging Potpourri Holder

This hanging potpourri holder makes a closet smell great.

Here is what you need:

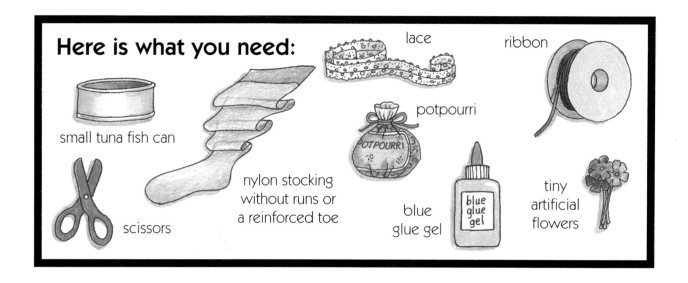

- small tuna fish can
- scissors
- nylon stocking without runs or a reinforced toe
- lace
- potpourri
- blue glue gel
- ribbon
- tiny artificial flowers

Here is what you do:

Fill the tuna can almost to the top with potpourri. Slide the can into the foot of the stocking. Pull the stocking tightly around the can so that the can is pushed all the way down into the toe. Tie the opening of the stocking in a tight knot on the side of the can. Trim off the excess stocking.

Glue lace around the edge of the opening of the can.

Hint: Blue glue gel will make this easier to do, but white glue will also work.

Tie a ribbon around the outside of the can and tie some little flowers to the can. Tie the two ends of the ribbon together to make a hanger for the can.

If you can find lots of fresh flowers, you may want to try making your own potpourri. I think roses, violets, and lilacs smell especially nice, but try different flowers until you find your own favorites.

You will need to dry the flowers by tying three or four stems together and hanging them upside down in a dry place. Mix the dried flower petals and small flower heads to create a blend of scents. You can also add a few drops of perfume if you know a grownup who is willing to let you have some.

41

oilet Tissue Cover

A large oatmeal box fits perfectly over a wrapped roll of toilet tissue, making it the perfect base for this attractive bathroom accessory.

Here is what you need:

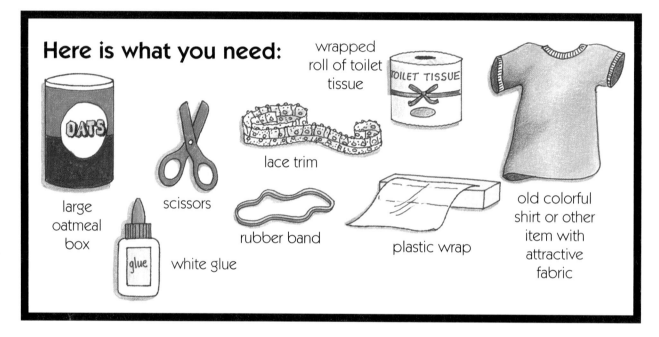

large oatmeal box

scissors

white glue

lace trim

rubber band

wrapped roll of toilet tissue

plastic wrap

old colorful shirt or other item with attractive fabric

Here is what you do:

Cut the bottom off the oatmeal box so that the bottom is the same height as the roll of toilet tissue.

Hint: Make sure that your wrapped roll of toilet tissue fits inside your oatmeal box. Different brands have small size variations that could make a difference.

Hint: If you are not skilled using scissors, ask an adult to help you. I always cut my boxes a little bigger than I need to, then I trim the edges to fit exactly.

Turn the bottom of the oatmeal box upside down. Cut a square of fabric large enough to cover the top and sides of the upside-down box with fabric to spare.

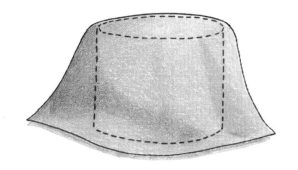

Hint: You need to use a fairly dark colored fabric so that the lettering on the sides of the box doesn't show through. I used an old green T-shirt to make my project, and it was very easy to work with and looks great. If you want to use a light-colored fabric, be sure to cover the sides of the box with white construction paper first.

Put a rubber band around the covered box to hold the fabric in place. Trim off all the extra fabric, leaving about 1 inch (2.5 centimeters) of extra fabric all the way around.

Cover the wrapped toilet tissue with plastic wrap. Rub glue all the way around the inside of the opening of the box. Tuck the ends of the fabric into the glued inside edge of the box. Slide the plastic-covered toilet tissue partway into the box to hold the fabric in place while the glue dries. When the project is dry, remove the wrapped tissue. Take the gluey plastic off of the tissue and throw it away.

Glue a band of lace around the top and the bottom of the holder to decorate it. Slip this pretty cover over the roll of toilet tissue, and this gift is complete.

43

Shoe Shine Kit

This shoe shine holder will help someone organize all the items needed for shoe care. The six compartments offer plenty of room for brushes, rags, and a variety of shoe polishes.

Here is what you need:

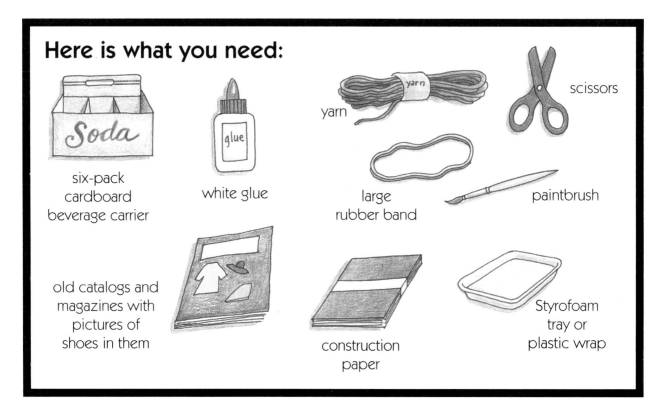

six-pack cardboard beverage carrier

white glue

yarn

large rubber band

scissors

paintbrush

old catalogs and magazines with pictures of shoes in them

construction paper

Styrofoam tray or plastic wrap

Here is what you do:

Cut construction paper to cover the sides and bottom of the cardboard beverage carrier. Cover the sides and bottom completely with a thin coat of glue. Glue the paper in place. If needed, put a rubber band around the outside of the carrier to hold the paper in place until the glue dries. Dry the project on plastic wrap or a Styrofoam tray.

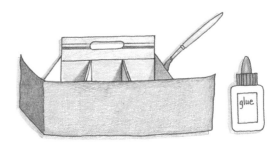

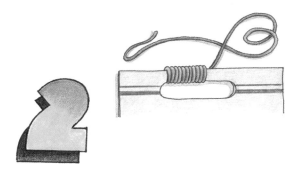

Cut a long piece of yarn. Cover the top part of the handle opening with glue. Tie one end of the yarn to the far side of one end of the handle opening. Wrap the entire handle with yarn. When you reach the other side of the handle with the yarn, cut off the extra yarn. Tuck the cut end under the wrapped yarn so that the glue under the yarn will hold it.

Cut out lots of pictures of shoes from the old magazines and catalogs. Use the pictures to make a collage of shoes on the sides of the carrier. You could ask around for some old T-shirts to cut into soft rags and include those in the carrier also.

What other kinds of containers could you make using a beverage carrier? How about one for cleaning supplies or sewing sup-plies? Maybe you should make one for yourself to keep your craft supplies in!

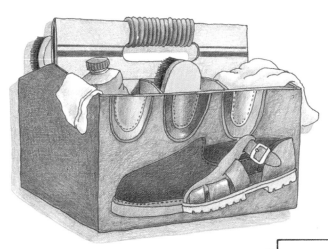

Powder Sachet and Cedar Envelope

Here are ideas for making two different kinds of sachets. The first one smells very pretty and is perfect for tucking into a drawer. The second one smells like cedar and will not only make a drawer smell pleasant, it will also help keep moths away from wool clothing.

Here is what you need:

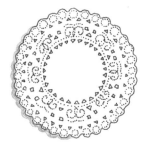

two 5-inch (13-centimeter) doilies

small envelope

nice-smelling dusting powder

two pretty pictures cut from old wallpaper or greeting cards

cellophane tape

white glue

Here is what you do:

1. Fill the envelope about half full with powder. Do not put in so much powder that you puff out the envelope. It should be fairly flat. Seal the envelope and tape the seams so that the powder does not leak out.

2. Center one of the doilies on the envelope and glue it in place. Glue the picture you have chosen in the center of the doily. Do the same thing on the other side of the envelope.

When the glue has dried, this pretty little package will be ready to give to someone on your gift list. It is so pretty it doesn't even need wrapping.

Here is what you need:

cedar block

white glue

scissors

hole punch

small note-card-size envelope

cellophane tape

yarn

Here is what you do:

Put the cedar block inside the envelope. Seal the envelope. If you wish you can also tape the flap shut to make sure it will stay closed.

Hint: Cedar blocks are available in most supermarkets and drugstores. My package had four blocks in it, so I made four cedar envelopes at the same time.

Punch holes spaced 1 inch (2.5 centimeters) apart all the way around the envelope. Cut a long piece of yarn. Tie and knot one end through a corner hole. Wrap tape around the other end of the yarn to make it stiff. This will make it easier to lace around the envelope. Lace the yarn all the way around the envelope until you are at the hole where you started. Tie and knot the end of the yarn through the same hole you started with, then cut off the extra yarn and the tape.

If you already have decided who you are going to give this to, put yarn initials of the person on the envelope. Shape the letters you need with pieces of yarn and glue them in place.

If you would like the cedar envelope to hang in a closet instead of being tucked in a drawer, tie a loop of yarn to one corner for hanging.

Pantyhose Holder

This easily constructed gift would be very useful to all the women on your gift list. Make this unique holder for one person, and I'll bet you will have other people asking you for one, too. It is so handy!

Here is what you need:

white glue

large Styrofoam tray or plastic wrap

lace trim

four square tissue boxes in pretty patterns

Here is what you do:

Stack the four boxes on their sides, so that two are on the bottom and two are on the top, with all four openings facing you. Put glue between all the sides that touch to keep the boxes stacked. Let the boxes dry completely on a large Styrofoam tray or on plastic wrap.

The boxes form four small compartments that will each hold several pairs of pantyhose. Lay the holder down so the openings are on top and run a line of glue all the way around the side with the four openings. Stick lace around the outer edge of the four compartments.

Before you give this gift away, tuck a package of pantyhose in one compartment to show what the holder is used for. Or include a note that explains how to use this gift.

What else could you use a holder like this for? You could make one with more compartments if you wanted to.

Gifts of Jewelry and Personal Decoration

Scrunchies

Scrunchies are elasticized bands that women of all ages like to wear in their hair or on their wrists. Beautiful scrunchies can be made from old neckties.

Here is what you need:

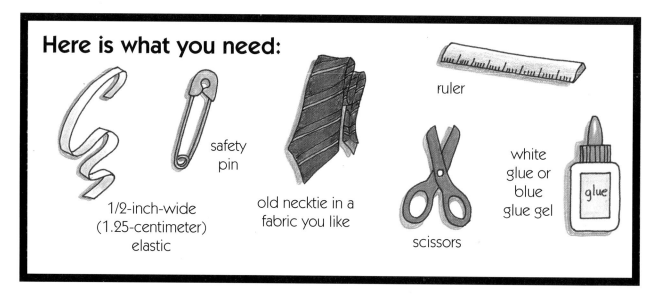

safety pin

ruler

1/2-inch-wide (1.25-centimeter) elastic

old necktie in a fabric you like

scissors

white glue or blue glue gel

glue

Here is what you do:

Cut a piece of elastic 8 inches (20 centimeters) long. Pin a safety pin to one end of the elastic.

Cut the necktie in half. You will use the narrow half of the tie for this project. Cut off the point of the tie. Trim the tie so that you have a strip 12 inches to 16 inches (30 centimeters to 40 centimeters) long.

Hint: Some people like scrunchies with lots of fabric in them. Experiment to see how much fabric you want. Remember, it is easier to start with a longer piece of fabric and trim off what you don't need. If the fabric you cut is too short, you may have to start over.

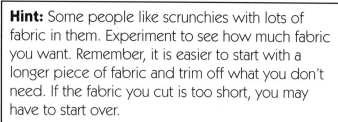

 Thread the safety pin on one end of the elastic through the necktie, bunching the fabric together over the elastic as you go.

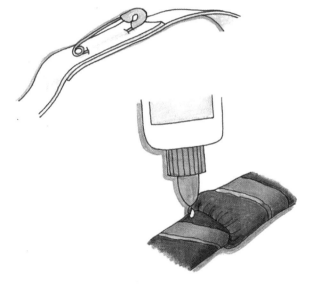

 Pin the two ends of the elastic together. Wrap the safety pin with masking tape to make sure that it will not open. Turn one of the open ends of the tie inside to create a clean edge, then slide that end over the other end of the tie about 1/2 inch (1.25 centimeters). Put a dab of glue between the two overlapping ends to secure them.

You can use these steps to make a headband, too. Cut a piece of elastic about 18 inches to 20 inches (45 centimeters to 50 centimeters) long, depending on the size of the person you are making the headband for. Thread the elastic through the thin end of a necktie. The strip of tie should be 4 inches (10 centimeters) longer than your elastic.

Be sure to save the rest of the necktie to make the Glasses Holder on page 62.

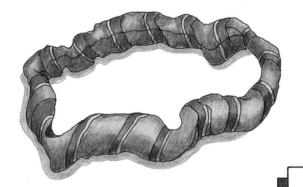

nimal Cracker Necklace

These animal cracker necklaces are as much fun to make as they are to wear. Buy a box of animal crackers and choose one or more unbroken crackers to make into necklaces. Once the box is open, you might as well eat the rest of the cookies. The crackers won't stay fresh for long.

Here is what you need:

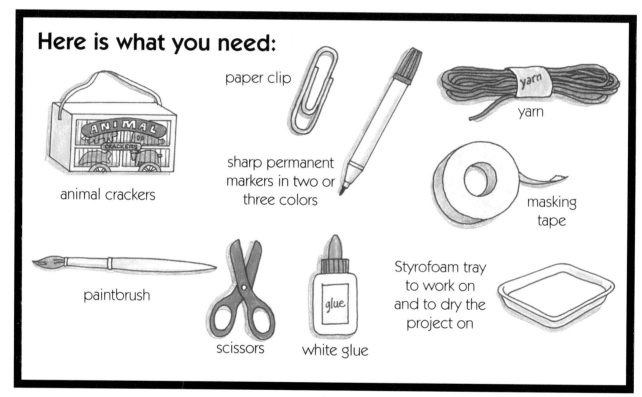

paper clip

sharp permanent markers in two or three colors

animal crackers

yarn

masking tape

paintbrush

scissors

white glue

Styrofoam tray to work on and to dry the project on

Here is what you do:

Carefully color the animal cracker with permanent markers.

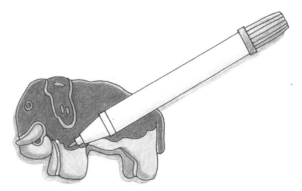

Coat the front of the cracker with glue to protect it. Let the project dry completely on a Styrofoam tray before you continue. When the front is dry, coat the back and edges with glue and let them dry.

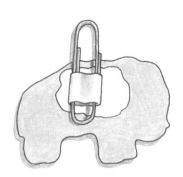

 To make a hanger for the necklace, wrap the bottom of a paper clip in masking tape. Glue the taped paper clip to the back of the cracker with the top loop of the clip sticking out over the top front of the cracker. Cut a long piece of yarn to string through the paper clip and tie the two ends of the yarn together to make a necklace.

> **Hint:** I have tried to color the cracker with regular markers, but the color ran when I later added the glue. If you use regular markers, be very careful when you paint the glue on and do not use too much.

Animal crackers do not make good pins because they'll crack and break as the pin is opened and closed. They do make nice magnets, though. Glue a piece of magnetic strip to the back of the cracker. Do not press on a piece of sticky-back magnet because the pressure of pressing might break the cracker.

Spaghetti Pin

Spaghetti to wear?

Here is what you need:

cardboard

disposable plastic tub with lid

spoon to mix with

pin backing

food coloring

paintbrush

scissors

masking tape

white glue

uncooked spaghetti

two Styrofoam trays

Here is what you do:

 Cut a small simple shape from the cardboard, 2 inches to 3 inches (5 centimeters to 8 centimeters) long.

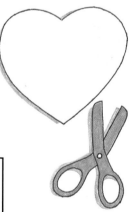

Hint: An egg shape or a heart shape is a good one to start with. Once you know how to make this project, you might try a more complicated shape, such as a leaf.

 Pour about 1/4 cup (50 milliliters) of white glue into a plastic tub and color the glue by mixing in two or three drops of food coloring.

Hint: This glue will dry several shades darker than it looks when it is still wet, so don't use more than two or three drops of food coloring. You could also simply use store-bought colored glue.

Working on one of the Styrofoam trays, paint the cardboard shape with colored glue. Break about ten sticks of spaghetti into thirds. Cover the entire shape with spaghetti sticks. Do not try to make the spaghetti fit the shape. You will trim around the shape later. Cover the spaghetti with glue so that it is completely colored. Let the project dry on a clean Styrofoam tray.

> **Hint:** Be sure to put the lid on your extra glue and save it. You might need it again. Please wash the spoon immediately!

When the glue is dry, use scissors to carefully trim around the edge of the cardboard shape to remove the extra spaghetti. If there are spots where the spaghetti broke off of the shape, use the trimmings and some of the colored glue to repair them. Let the glue dry again before you continue to the next step.

 Wrap a small amount of masking tape around the base of the pin backing to help the glue stick. Glue the pin to the back of the spaghetti-covered shape and hold it in place with a piece of masking tape. When the glue has dried, this pin is ready to wear.

If you would like to write a message on the spaghetti pin, use white glue to attach macaroni alphabet letters. When the glue has dried, cover the letters with a thin coating of white glue to protect them.

Spaghetti shapes can also be used as magnets. Just add a piece of sticky-back magnet to the back instead of a pin.

Necktie House Pin

This charming little house pin is a quick and easy gift to make when you need something nice in a hurry.

Here is what you need:

old necktie

felt scraps in different colors

cotton

sharp black marker or pen

Styrofoam tray to dry the project on

safety pin

white glue

yarn and other trims

scissors

Here is what you do:

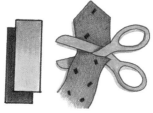

1 For each house you want to make, cut a 2-inch (5-centimeter) piece from the thin end of the tie. This will give you a square house shape with a pointed roof.

2 Cut tiny doors, windows, and a chimney from colored felt scraps. Draw on doorknobs and window panes with the marker. Glue the pieces in place on the house. Glue a piece of yarn or trim across the point between the square house shape and the roof. Puff out a tiny piece of cotton to glue behind the chimney to look like smoke coming out.

3 If the back of the tie is no longer stitched together, glue the two flaps down. Let the house dry on a Styrofoam tray. Pin a safety pin to the back of the house, and it will be ready to wear. Necktie houses also make very nice refrigerator magnets. Instead of putting a safety pin on the back, attach a piece of sticky-back magnet.

Gifts to

Use Around

the House

Packing Tape Bookmark

Make designer bookmarks for all the readers on your gift list.

Here is what you need:

roll of clear packing tape, 2 inches (5 centimeters) wide

small pressed flowers

glitter

stickers

scissors

yarn

hole punch

Here is what you do:

Carefully tear off a piece of tape about 16 inches (40 centimeters) long and lay it on a flat nonstick surface such as a countertop, with the sticky side up.

Hint: You can easily press flowers by folding them in a paper towel and placing them between the pages of a heavy book for several days. Be sure that the flowers are dry and that you use a paper towel so that you do not mark the book pages. Small dried leaves and clover would also work well for this project.

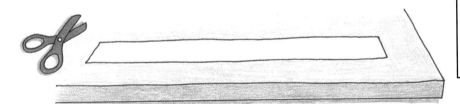

Arrange your flowers, some face down and some face up, on about 8 inches (20 centimeters) of the tape. Remember that this bookmark has two sides, and you will want both sides to look pretty.

Hint: Be sure to work carefully, because tape sticks to itself very easily. The first time I tried this, I was not careful and had to throw the strip away and try again.

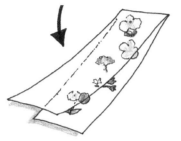

Again being careful, fold the tape in half and stick the two halves together with the flowers in the middle. If the edges don't match up exactly after you have stuck the tape together, you can trim off any extra tape.

The folded end of the tape will be the top of the bookmark. Cut the opposite end of the bookmark into a point. Punch a hole in the point and tie two 5-inch (13-centimeter) pieces of yarn through the hole to make a tassel.

What else could you put inside the tape to make a pretty design? I made one with glitter and sticker stars that was very pretty. (I also made one with colored glue in the middle, but the glue never dried!) You could cut shapes from colored construction paper or punch them with a shape hole punch. Shapes from colored paper work well because they look nice on both sides. Don't be afraid to experiment. Lots of my ideas do not work out, but I get very excited over the ones that do!

atchbox Drawers

This tabletop chest of drawers is just right for storing small items. It is useful on a dresser or desktop and makes an attractive gift.

Here is what you need:

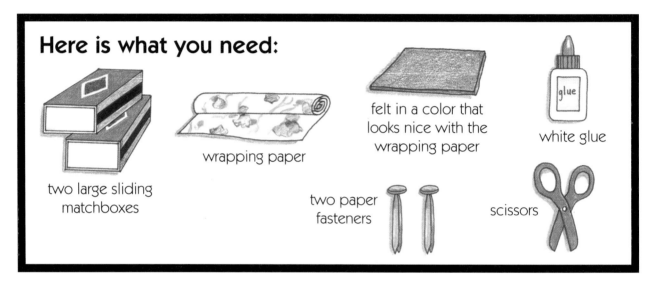

two large sliding matchboxes

wrapping paper

felt in a color that looks nice with the wrapping paper

white glue

two paper fasteners

scissors

Here is what you do:

Remove the inner boxes from the matchboxes. Stack the two remaining outer matchboxes one on top of the other and glue them together. Cut the wrapping paper to cover the outsides of the boxes, folding it over one of the open ends as you would when wrapping a present. Glue the paper in place and glue the folded end shut. Cut a square of paper to cover the folded end. Glue the square in place.

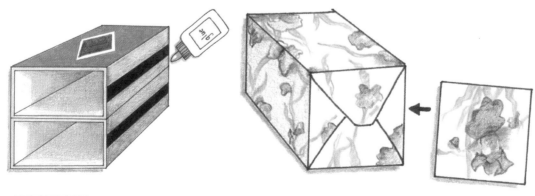

 The inner boxes will be the drawers. Cover the front of each drawer with felt. Cut a piece of felt to line the inside bottom of each drawer and glue the felt in place.

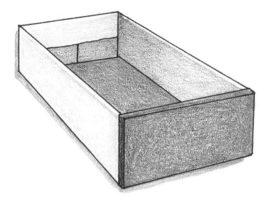

Hint: The paper that you choose to cover the drawers will depend upon the person who will be getting the gift. You might choose a flowery print for one person, but an old road map or calendar for another person. Use your imagination. Think about the person you are making this gift for and choose just the right covering for that person.

Poke a paper fastener through the felt on the front of each drawer to use as a drawer pull.

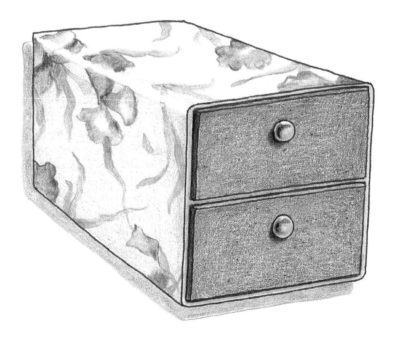

Experiment with making a larger set of drawers, either by stacking more boxes together or gluing two sets side by side.

Glasses Holder

You can make beautiful eyeglass cases from old neckties. These cases will be as varied as the fabrics of the old neckties you are able to collect.

Here is what you need:

old necktie

scissors

blue glue gel

set of sticky-backed Velcro dots

Here is what you do:

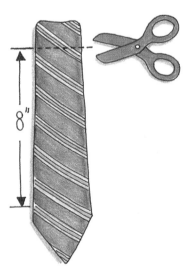

8"

Cut an 8-inch-long (20-centimeter) piece off the wide end of the tie. Do not include the triangle-shaped part that forms the point when you are measuring.

Hint: Make sure the necktie is wide enough to fit a pair of eyeglasses into. Some glasses won't fit in a narrow-style tie.

Hint: White glue will also work with this project, but you will need to be careful not to let it run on the tie because it will leave a dark stain when it dries.

If the tie has a tag on the inside, carefully remove it. If the seam of the tie is starting to unravel, close the seam with blue glue gel. Fold the edges of the flat open ends into the tie and glue the opening shut.

Hint: If the opening won't stay shut, use clothespins or paper clips to hold it together until the glue dries.

 Press on two sticky-backed Velcro dots—one on the triangle point and one on the tie—to make a fastener. To close the case, simply fold the triangle over.

You can use this same idea to make a smaller change purse or earring case. Just cut a 6-inch (15-centimeter) piece off the wide end of the tie, without including the point in your measurement. Fold the tie over on itself and glue the sides together. What other kind of case could you make? How about a scissors holder for your craft scissors?

Matchbox Sewing Kit

This tiny sewing kit fits nicely in a pocket or purse, ready to be of use when the owner needs it most.

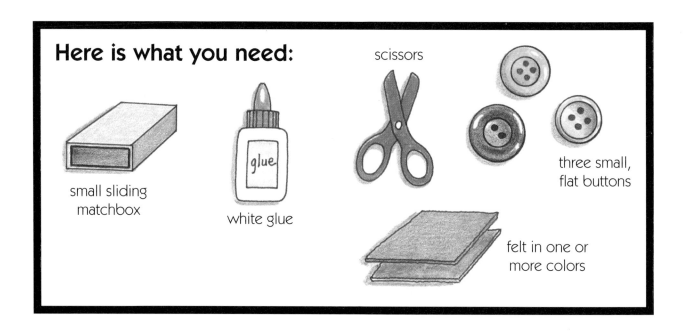

Here is what you need:

small sliding matchbox

white glue

scissors

three small, flat buttons

felt in one or more colors

Here is what you do:

Cut a piece of felt to fit around the out-side of the matchbox. It should fit exact-ly, without overlapping, so that you won't have a bump on one side of the box. Glue the felt on the box.

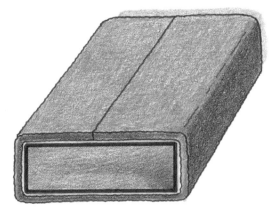

Arrange the three buttons on the top of the box and glue them on.

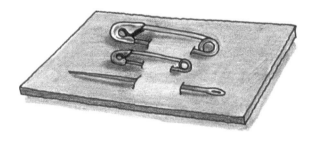

 Cut a piece of felt to fit inside the box to keep needles and pins on.

If you would like to fill the sewing kit here are some suggestions for things you might want to include.

- A piece of thin cardboard with a long piece of white thread wrapped around one end and a long piece of black thread wrapped around the other end.
- Two or three different sizes and colors of buttons.
- Two safety pins of different sizes, pinned to the felt square.
- A sewing needle and some straight pins pinned through the felt square.

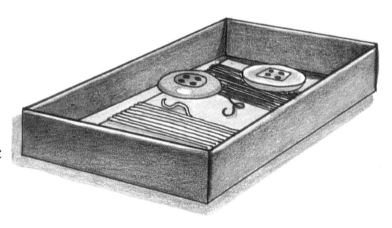

What other kind of emergency box could you make using this idea? Maybe you could make a box for spare change or use a larger kitchen matchbox to make a first aid kit. How would you decorate these two boxes to show what they are for?

65

irds Pin Cushion

This nest full of birds will be glad to keep track of pins for any grownup you know who likes to sew.

Here is what you need:

blue and yellow felt scraps

thin ribbon

plastic cap or detergent bottle top, at least 2 inches (5 centimeters) in diameter

old dark-colored knit glove

pen

cotton or fiberfill

masking tape

white glue

scissors

Here is what you do:

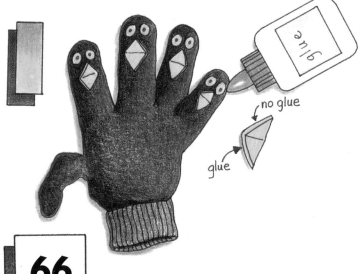

no glue

glue

glue

Stuff the four fingers and hand portion of the glove with cotton or fiberfill. Do not stuff the thumb of the glove. Each finger of the glove will be a bird. Cut a beak from yellow felt for each bird. Cut eyes for each bird from blue felt. Use a pen to put a pupil in the center of each eye. Glue two eyes and a beak on one side of each finger to give the birds faces.

66

 The plastic cap will be the birds' nest. Cover the inside of the cap with masking tape. Cover the tape inside the cap with glue. Stuff the bottom of the glove down into the cap making sure that the unstuffed thumb is tucked down into the cap also. The four birds should now look as though they are peeking out of the cap nest.

Tie a pretty ribbon around the outside rim of the cap.

You might want to include some pins with this gift to show what it is for. This charming pin cushion is much too nice to tuck away in a sewing kit. The lucky grownup who gets this gift will probably want to keep it on display.

67

Button Napkin Rings

Buttons are one of my favorite items to collect. There are so many different kinds. If you have a button collection, too, you might want to make a set of these napkin rings for someone.

Here is what you need:

at least twelve buttons for each ring

scissors

pipe cleaners

Here is what you do:

1. Cut a piece of pipe cleaner about 6 inches (15 centimeters) long. Choose an assortment of about twelve buttons that look nice together. String the buttons on the pipe cleaner, sliding them as close together as possible to cover the pipe cleaner.

2. Twist the two ends of the pipe cleaner together to shape the buttons into a ring about 2 inches (5 centimeters) across. Tuck the ends of the pipe cleaner in around the buttons so that you have a circle of evenly spaced buttons. Make a set of four or more of these rings to create this pleasing and useful gift for the table.

Hint: If you are using buttons with holes in the middle, you need to string the pipe cleaner in and out of the holes in each button.

Gifts for Decorating

Pasta Box Magnet

The windows on many pasta boxes make great frames for photographs or for your own artwork.

Here is what you need:

pencil

scissors

glue

white glue

photograph

pasta box with a
cellophane window

strip of sticky-
back magnet

Here is what you do:

Cut around the window of the pasta box so that you have a 1/4-inch to 1/2-inch (.5-centimeter to 1.25-centimeter) frame of cardboard around the cellophane window. Trace around the frame on a piece of the remaining box. Cut out the traced shape to use as a backing for the frame.

2 Choose a photo that has a subject that fits inside the frame window. Trace around the frame on the photograph and cut out the portion of the photo you are going to frame.

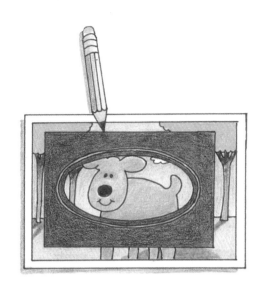

3 Glue the photograph over the writing side of the back piece of cardboard. Glue the frame over the front of the photograph. Press a piece of sticky-back magnet to the back of the frame.

You could make a set of these magnets in different sizes and wrap them together as a gift. You can also use just one as a little surprise to tuck in a letter or thank-you note.

Greeting Card Photo Frame

Many greeting ~~cards~~ have an attractive frame around the pictu... ...hat is just right for this project. Framed photos ...l gifts that are easily mailed in an en...

Here is ~~what y~~ou need:

- greeting card with a border
- photograph
- scissors
- yarn
- white glue
- eight paper clips

Here is what you do:

Cut the picture out of the inside of the greeting card without cutting apart the border. Poke a hole in the center to start the scissors.

Hint: Greeting cards and photographs come in a variety of sizes. Make sure that the greeting card you choose will create a frame with an opening that is slightly smaller than your photograph. It should cover the edges of the photo on all four sides. On the other hand, you may need to trim the photograph to fit the frame if the photograph is too big.

2 Cut a 5-inch (13-centimeter) piece of yarn to use as a hanger. Rub glue around the inside of the frame and the back inside of the card. Place the photograph in the frame with the bottom of the photograph toward the folded end of the card. Place the two ends of the yarn behind the photograph ⟨...⟩ ⟨...⟩ the card to stick everything together. ⟨...⟩ paper clips to hold the card shut ⟨...⟩ glue has dried.

Write a message on the back of the card and sign your name.

73

Rainbow Light Catcher

The vivid colors of this rainbow will look beautiful hanging in a window with the sun shining through them.

Here is what you need:

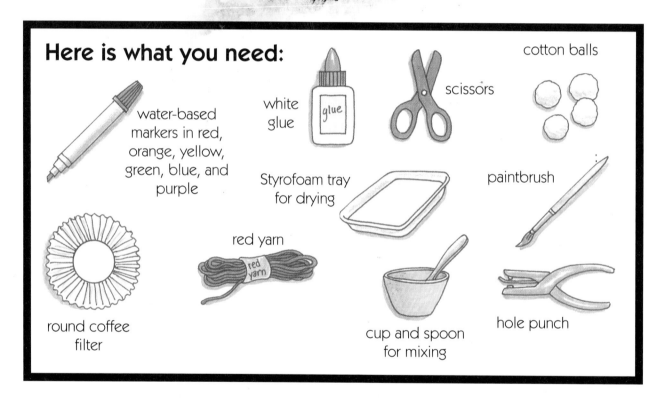

water-based markers in red, orange, yellow, green, blue, and purple

white glue

scissors

cotton balls

Styrofoam tray for drying

paintbrush

round coffee filter

red yarn

cup and spoon for mixing

hole punch

Here is what you do:

Cut the coffee filter in half. Cut the half circle from the center of one half so that you are left with an arch of paper.

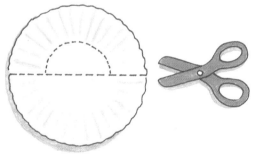

2 Use the markers to color the arch to look like a rainbow.

3 Pour about 2 tablespoons (25 milliliters) of glue into a cup. Thin the glue with 1 teaspoon (5 milliliters) of water. Mix the glue and water well.

4 Lay the rainbow on a Styrofoam tray. Paint over the rainbow with watery glue so that the colors run together and brighten. Let the rainbow dry stiff.

5 Fluff out some cotton balls to use as clouds. Glue them on each side of the two bottom ends of the rainbow. Poke a hole at the top of each side of the rainbow. Cut a long piece of yarn. Thread the ends through the two holes at the top of the rainbow. Tie the two ends of the yarn together to form a hanger.

Try coloring an uncut filter with random patches of color. Cut it into a shape such as a leaf or butterfly. Cover it with glue and let it dry. You can make all sorts of different sun catchers using this idea.

 ayered Beans Vase

This little vase of flowers would make a cheerful get-well gift for someone.

Here is what you need:

two colors of thin ribbon that look nice together

large baby food jar or other jar of similar size

artificial flowers

dried yellow peas or unpopped popcorn

dried green peas

rice

dried kidney beans

white glue

glue

scissors

Here is what you do:

Fill the jar one quarter full with the dried green peas. Gently shake the jar to help them settle evenly in the jar. Next add a layer of red beans to half fill the jar. Next add rice to the jar. Fill the remainder of the jar with the yellow peas or popcorn.

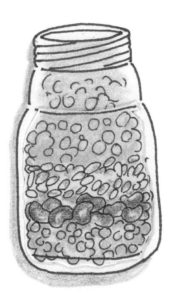

Plant the flowers by poking the stems carefully down into the layers of beans, disturbing the layers as little as possible. If the stems of the flowers are too long, trim them before you stick them in the jar.

 Squeeze white glue all over the top layer of beans around and in between the flowers. Let the glue dry hard to hold the layers of beans in the jar.

 Cut two pieces of ribbon and tie them together around the rim of the jar in a pretty bow.

You can layer the inside of the jar with any combination of beans and rice that you choose. You could also color some rice or sand with a few drops of food coloring. Be sure to let colored rice or sand dry overnight before you seal it in the jar. If you don't it might mold. YUCK!

Shredded Wheat Wreath

Breakfast cereal makes an unusual but very pretty door wreath!

Here is what you need:

paper plate

scissors

hole punch

green food coloring

yarn

paintbrush

white glue

bowl and spoon for mixing

three biscuits of Shredded Wheat cereal

styrofoam tray

Here is what you do:

Cut the center out of a paper plate to form a wreath shape. Punch a hole on the edge of the plate. Cut a 4-inch (10-centimeter) piece of yarn. Thread the yarn through the hole and tie the ends together to form a hanger for the wreath.

Hint: The glue will dry much darker than it appears when wet, so you don't need to add extra coloring to the glue to make it look darker.

78

Pour about 1 cup (250 milliliters) of glue into a bowl. Color the glue with about 1/2 teaspoon (2 milliliters) of green food coloring. Mix until the glue is evenly colored.

Hint: Store-bought green glue will also work with this project.

Turn the wreath so the outside edges are curved up. Paint all the way around the wreath with green glue.

Hint: If the mixture seems too dry, pour in a little more glue. If it seems too wet, shred some more cereal and add it to the mixture. The cereal should be totally green without a lot of extra glue left in the bottom of the bowl.

Crumble three biscuits of Shredded Wheat into the glue and mix until the cereal is evenly coated with green glue.

Pile the cereal mixture around the wreath frame to shape the wreath. You may not need to use all of the mixture. Stop when you think the plate looks evenly covered. Let this project dry on a Styrofoam tray.

You can decorate this wreath for the season in which you are giving it. If it is Christmas time, you might glue on some red beads to look like berries and add a pretty red bow. If it is springtime, you could glue on some small artificial flowers. I made one for Valentine's Day and glued on red paper hearts. Use one of these ideas or an idea of your own to decorate this wreath.

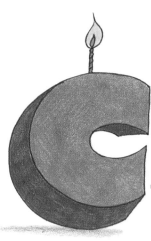

Candle Holder

A simple little jar can be turned into a lovely candle holder in no time at all.

Here is what you need:

short, wide candle

jar that the candle will fit in

salt

red or pink nail polish

Styrofoam tray to work on

thin pink or red ribbon

Hint: You might want to make a small paper stencil for the shape.

Here is what you do:

Use nail polish to paint a simple shape on each side of the jar.

Quickly sprinkle salt over each wet shape to make it glisten. Let the nail polish dry. Do one side at a time.

Tie a pretty ribbon around the neck of the jar. Put the candle inside the jar.
   Three of these candle holders together would make a very nice table arrangement.

Expandable Map Holder

This gift is used to keep car maps protected and together.

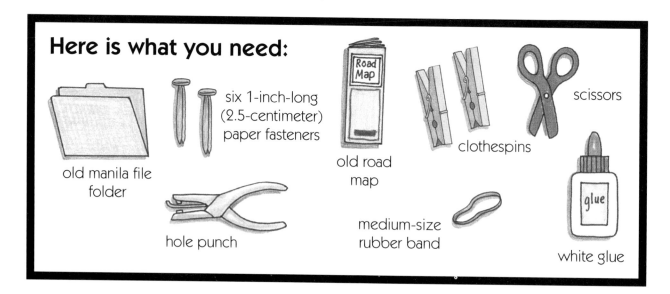
Here is what you do:

If the file folder has a tab on it, trim off the tab so that the edges of the folder are even. Open the folder and lay it down on your work surface with the outside of the folder facing up. Cover the entire outside of the folder with glue. Cover the folder with paper from an old road map, trimming off the extra paper so that it fits exactly.

While the glue is still wet, turn the folder over and fold the bottom and top of it to make an envelope with a flap. Hold the folder closed with clothespins until it dries.

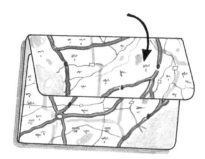

Hint: You will not be able to use the hole punch to make the last hole—it is too far from an edge of the folder. Ask an adult to poke the hole for you using the point of a sharp pair of scissors.

DON'T PUNCH THIS ONE THROUGH THE BACK OF THE FOLDER

 Punch a hole in the top and the bottom of each side of the folder. Punch a hole in the middle of the folder flap. Also poke a hole in the middle of the bottom half of the front of the folder, but not through the back.

 Put a paper fastener through each of the four holes on the sides of the folder. The fasteners can be folded tight to the folder if it is going to contain only one or two maps. If you want to make a larger folder that can fit more maps, just loosen the paper fasteners slightly on each side.

Put a fastener in the holes on the flap and bottom front of the folder. Slip the end of a rubber band over the paper fastener on the flap of the folder. To close the folder, just slip the other end of the rubber band over the second paper fastener.

What other kinds of folders could you make using this idea? How about a coupon folder or a greeting-card folder? What would you use to cover these folders to show how the folder is to be used?

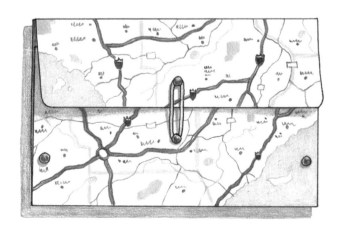

ar Litter Holder

Every car can use a container for litter. This box is especially useful for any grownup you know who might be planning a long trip.

Here is what you need:

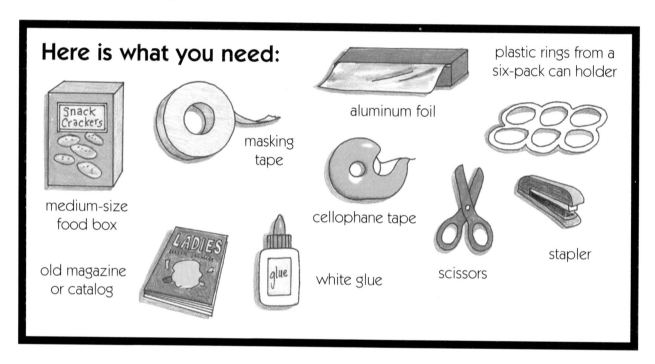

aluminum foil

plastic rings from a six-pack can holder

Snack Crackers

masking tape

cellophane tape

stapler

medium-size food box

old magazine or catalog

LADIES

glue

white glue

scissors

Here is what you do:

Cut the top flaps off the box so that the top of the box is open. Cover the box with aluminum foil, folding the foil over the bottom of the box just as you would when wrapping a present. Tuck the extra foil inside the box. Secure the seams and edges of the aluminum foil with cellophane tape.

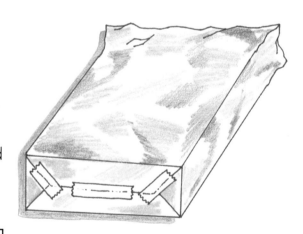

Hint: Snack-cracker boxes are just the right size for this project.

2 Cut one ring out of the six-pack holder. Make sure you don't cut through the ring. To make a hanger, staple the ring to the center of the opening on the outside back of the box.

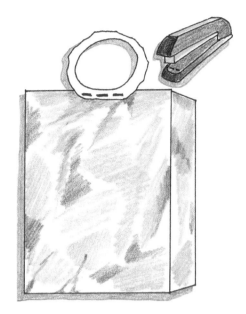

Cut letters that are about the same size out of an old magazine or catalog to spell the word "Litter." Put a strip of masking tape across the front of the box. Glue the letters on the masking tape.

Hint: If you try to glue the letters directly on the foil, they will not stick well. You need the masking tape to provide a good sticking surface for the white glue.

If you wish, put a small plastic bag inside the litter holder to make emptying it easier. You could include some extra bags with this gift if you want to. Just tuck them inside the box.

ar-Care Rag Bag

If you know someone who is always washing the car, this is the gift to give. This bag hangs in the garage or cellar, full of rags to use for washing and waxing the car.

Here is what you need:

 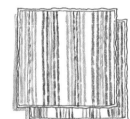

yarn or string

scissors

two identical loose-weave dish rags

Here is what you do:

Cut a piece of yarn that will be long enough to sew around three sides of the dish rags. Hold the two cloths exactly together. Tie one end of the yarn through the two cloths at one of the corners. Lace the yarn in and out around three sides of both cloths to sew them together. Tie off the yarn and trim off any extra yarn.

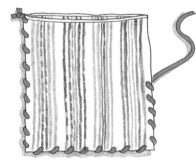

Hint: To make the lacing easier, tape the end of the yarn to make it stiff. You could also dip the end of the yarn in glue and let it dry to stiffen it.

Cut a long piece of yarn. Tie one end to each side of the open end of the bag to make a hanger.

Collect some soft old undershirts and cut them into squares to use as a filler to show what this bag is for.

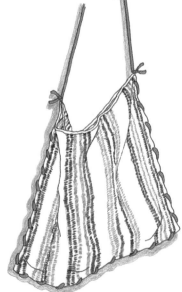

Gifts of

Food

Orange Tea Mix

This orange tea mix would make a delicious gift for a grownup who likes to drink tea.

Here is what you need:

measuring cups for dry ingredients

package of orange gelatin

ORANGE GELATIN

unsweetened powdered instant tea

INSTANT TEA

sugar

mixing bowl and spoon

Here is what you do:

Measure 1 cup (250 milliliters) of instant tea and pour it into the bowl. Measure 1/2 cup (125 milliliters) of sugar and pour it into the bowl.

2 Add one package of orange gelatin and mix until everything is well blended.

3 To make orange tea, add 2 tablespoons (25 milliliters) of tea mix to 6 ounces (187 milliliters) of hot water and stir.

That's it! Your own orange tea mix is ready to package for gift giving.

If you are going to give all the tea mix to one person, put it in a zip-to-close plastic bag. You might want to cut some shapes or the letters to spell "tea" from scraps of Con-Tact paper. Use these or stickers to decorate the plastic bag. Remember to write the mixing instructions on a card or sticky label and include them with the mix.

If you want to give away individual servings of tea mix, measure 2 tablespoons (25 milliliters) of mix and put it in a zip-to-close plastic sandwich bag. Decorate an envelope and write the mixing instructions on the front. Put the bag of tea in the envelope.

Chocolate Coated Spoons

Licking one of these spoons after it has been dipped in a hot drink of cocoa or coffee is pure pleasure for any chocolate lover.

Here is what you need:

chocolate chips

two plastic spoons

spoon

measuring spoons

solid shortening

measuring cup

small microwave-safe coffee cup

two drinking glasses to dry spoons on

Here is what you do:

Pour 1/4 cup (50 milliliters) of chocolate chips into the cup. Add 1 1/2 teaspoons (7 milliliters) of shortening.

Hint: This gift can also be made with real spoons if you have any you want to give away.

Microwave the mixture on high for one minute, then stir. Continue to microwave until the chocolate chips are melted. Stir the melted mixture thoroughly.

Hint: If you are not yet allowed to use the microwave, ask an adult to do this for you. If you do not have a microwave, melt the chocolate chips and shortening in the top of a double boiler on the stove. You will definitely need an adult to do this.

Use the mixing spoon to spoon the chocolate over the front and back of the bowl of one of the plastic spoons. Carefully set the spoon across the rim of a glass to dry, disturbing as little of the chocolate surface as possible. Do the same with the second spoon. The chocolate will dry hard in about ten minutes.

These spoons are best to give away when they are freshly made. They will sometimes discolor after several days. Put the two spoons in a plastic bag, chocolate end first. Tie a ribbon around the bag, part way up the handles of the spoons, to close the bag.

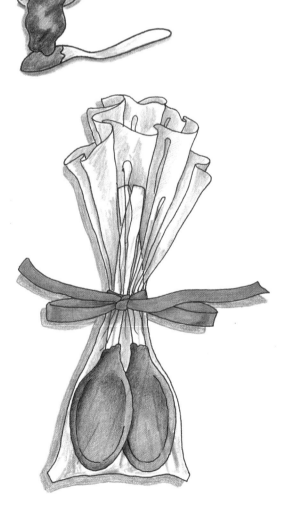

91

ocha Drink Mix

Mocha drink mix makes a delicious gift. You can give part of this mix away and save some for yourself.

Here is what you need:

mixing bowl and spoon

measuring cups for dry ingredients

measuring spoons

powdered milk

cinnamon

baking cocoa

instant coffee

sugar

Here is what you do:

Measure 1 cup (250 milliliters) of powdered milk into the bowl. Add 1 cup of sugar. Add 1/4 cup (50 milliliters) of instant coffee. Add 1/2 cup (125 milliliters) of baking cocoa.

Add 1/2 teaspoon (2 milliliters) of cinnamon.

MILK SUGAR COFFEE COCOA

Mix all the ingredients together until they are well blended.

To make a mocha drink, mix 5 teaspoons (20 milliliters) of mix into 1 cup (250 milliliters) of hot water and stir well.

If you are planning to give all of the mix away, you will need a can with a lid, such as a coffee can, to put the mix in. Cover the can with pretty wallpaper or wrapping paper or a piece of paper that you have decorated yourself. You will need to write out the instructions for using the mix on a small piece of paper and tape it on the front of the can. If you wish, you could tie two or three Chocolate-Coated Spoons to the can (page 88).

If you would like to give away individual servings of mocha drink mix, measure one serving into a zip-to-close plastic bag. Fold the bag and slide it into a 4 1/2-inch (11-centimeter) cardboard tube. Wrap the tube with colored tissue paper and tie both ends closed with pretty ribbon. Write the mixing instructions on the side of the tube.

Mocha Drink Mix
Add 5 heaping teaspoons of mix to hot water and stir.

Mocha Drink Mix
Add contents to one cup of hot water and stir

ean Soup Mix

This decorated jar can be used to store dry beans and other dry foods after the bean soup mix is used up.

Here is what you need:

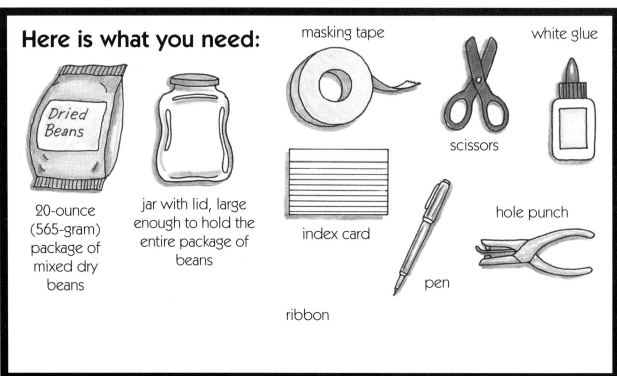

20-ounce (565-gram) package of mixed dry beans

jar with lid, large enough to hold the entire package of beans

masking tape

index card

scissors

white glue

hole punch

pen

ribbon

Here is what you do:

Soak the jar to remove the label. Wash the jar.

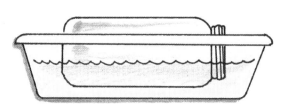

> **Hint:** Running the jar through the dishwasher will usually remove the label easily.

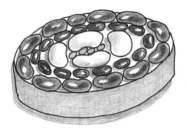

To decorate the lid of the jar, you will need to cover the lid with masking tape. Use some of the beans from the package to make a pretty design on top of the lid. Glue the beans on the lid.

Hint: You might want to glue the beans with colored glue to make a bright background on the lid.

Cover the edge of the lid with glue, then cover the glue with ribbon.

Write the recipe below on an index card or make a photocopy.

Punch a hole in the corner of the index card and tie it to the neck of the jar with ribbon.

Your family might have a different recipe for bean soup that you could use instead of the one given here.

 Bean Soup

Soak all the beans in cold water overnight. Drain the beans and simmer them in 3 quarts (3 liters) of fresh water for one hour.

Add 1/2 cup (125 milliliters) each of chopped celery, carrots, and onions.

Add one 16-ounce (500-milliliter) can of chopped tomatoes.

Add 1 tablespoon (15 milliliters) of lemon juice, 2 tablespoons (30 milliliters) of Worcestershire sauce, 1 tablespoon of dried basil, 1 teaspoon (5 milliliters) of garlic powder, and 1/2 teaspoon (2 milliliters) of black pepper.

Again, simmer for one hour.

Add 1/2 pound (225 grams) of sliced kielbasa and 1 cup (250 milliliters) of cut-up chicken.

Simmer for one more hour.

Serve with parmesan cheese or hot sauce. This soup is also very good over rice.

95

About the author and illustrator

Twenty years as a teacher and director of nursery school programs have given Kathy Ross extensive experience in guiding young children through crafts projects. She is the author of the eight-book series, Holiday Crafts for Kids, published by The Millbrook Press.

Anne Canevari Green has illustrated more than fifty books for young readers. She and her husband, Monte, live and work in a seaside cottage in Westhampton Beach, Long Island, New York. Anne says that Monte is <u>her</u> favorite grownup.